Marking the Hours

A Collection of Poems

Lenora Rain-Lee Good

"There is no death. Only a change of worlds."

—Si'ahl (Seattle), Suquamish Chief

For Thomas Hubbard,
a remarkable poet
who, through the years,
has been most generous
with his help,
his encouragement,
and his friendship.

Thank you.

Contents

My Dream of Heaven

I died in my dream
went to Heaven
where our ancestors
met me, welcomed me,
including our Anointed one
who wanted
to save his people
was meant
to save all people
who, like his cousin
two thousand years before him
died
by violence from those
who did not understand
who did not know
who did not care
who rammed bayonets
into his body
until he breathed his last.

Like the one before him
Crazy Horse forgave—
forgave their actions
forgave their ignorance.
In my dream
he opened his arms wide
smiled, said
Aho Mitakuye Oyasin.
I awoke to his embrace.

Aho Mitakuye Oyasin: Lakota for "Yes, we are all related."

2,075 Possible Tickets to Eternity

(28 January 1986, disintegration of STS-51-L)

We told our children
their end was quick
that they walked
with angels in just a
breath of
anticipation.

> T minus 2:03. Astronaut Judith A. Resnik:
> *[It's my] "security blanket."*

That lie, uttered in
innocence, meant
to save our children
pain and nightmares
now lays
shattered
at the feet of God.

> T minus 1:04. United States Air Force Lieutenant Colonel
> Ellison Onizuka:
> *"Dick's thinking
> of somebody there."*

Our government
in its dialectic speed
eventually found
answers
none too
pleasant.

T minus 0:25. Navy Commander Michael J. Smith:
"Remember the red button
when you make a roll call."

T minus 0:06. Mission Commander Francis R. Scobee:
"There they go, guys."
(ignition)

They
cheered and urged
her onward
upward to
freedom.

T plus 0:15. Judy Resnik:
(expletive) "hot!"

Into the vacuum
toward the stars.

T plus 0:28, Commander Smith:
"There's 10,000 feet and
mach point five."

Trained, professional,
the seven fought
to live —
they worked controls
gulped their
two minutes of emergency air
prepared
to meet their God
at splashdown

T plus 0:60, Commander Smith:
"Feel that mother go!"
T plus 0:60, Uncertain:
"Woooohoooo!"

A flash of fire
and seven fell to
the stars above.
Our only good-bye a short...

"Uh-oh"

At T plus 1:13, by Commander Smith

They flew above a
bomb—built by the lowest
bidder.
Only 2,075
possible quality
control problems.

"We have a major malfunction"
SAID THE TELEVISION VOICE

Inspired by the television coverage and the Challenger Transcript released by NASA and published in *Aviation Week and Space Technology*, August 4, 1986, page 37. The bracket phrase is the authors.) NOTE: I read the transcript in Aviation Week, a paywalled magazine, that may have been somewhat condensed; the full transcript is at: https://history.nasa.gov/transcript.html

I No Longer Visit the South

I don't know how to hug a ghost.
I no longer visit the South.
I no longer visit New Orleans—
too many ghosts weep, too many
ghosts moan and wail

too many ghosts see me
know me, come to me.
When I was nine
I strolled the French Quarter
with my grandparents.

The ghosts came to me, unbidden.
They appeared as shimmery shadows,
not quite there, not quite seen,
but felt, experienced. Their cries
a whispered agony against my skin.

Unseen, unheard by my grandparents
I saw. I heard. Especially the mothers
and the children separated
at the slave block where they were
sold, bought. The pain too much

for them, for me. Ghosts of the enslaved
still come when I visit the South.
I hear their cries, feel their pain and
open my arms to hold them but
I don't know how to hold a ghost.

Why do they choose me? I do not know.
We are all related, do they see how?
I hear them but cannot understand their words.
The ghosts at one old plantation
just around the bend of the river,
forbade my entrance, stole my voice
when I crossed their river to visit.
I drove past, visited the nearby town,
had lunch, wondered why?

Two hours later, when I returned
they gave my voice back. Did they use it
to speak to someone with ears to hear? I hope so.
I asked their names
I could not understand their answers

I asked for their stories
I could not understand their replies
I don't know how to hold a ghost.
I no longer visit the South.
I now ask that they please be at peace.

Be at peace, you are remembered.
Be at peace, accept my love.
Be at peace, accept my hug.
Be at peace, be at peace.
It is time—be at peace.

Mary Oliver Wants to Die When it's Raining

Mary Oliver wants to die
when it's raining—a long, slow rain,
a kind that may never end,
like I used to imagine
on Venus, until science
dissolved that dream in a
cloud of sulfuric acid.

I think I want to die
in the Spring, when
the sun is light and warm,
when the birds are loud
and raucous, when the trees
outside my window
burst with new life
as mine fades.

Unless I die in Summer
when starving baby birds screech,
when gossipy mosquitoes annoy
with their whiny high-pitched stories,
when children run, shriek
with laughter, through
sprinklers outside my window,
when night comes soft as my
lover's caress.

Perhaps I want to die in Autumn,
watching the trees outside my

window go from green to gold
to red to bare, hear footsteps crunch
dry leaves randomly scattered on the ground,
when stars are so bright
sleep is hard to come by.

No. Wait. I think I want to die
in Winter. Quiet Winter—sparkling
white with snow. Short days, long
nights, naked trees outside
my window with
playful squirrels searching
the diamonds of sun on
snow for seeds, and finding only
tangible cold. Quiet. Winter.
I'll slip away, be gone
before anyone sees, ride
the back of Brother Owl
into the cold and sparkling night.

I don't suppose
it matters. I will die when
Death calls for me and
not a day sooner. His
timing will be perfect—as long
as it's next season.

After "Marengo" by Mary Oliver

All My Relations

I can't breathe,
the last words
spoken by my uncle as
he lay dying of cancer.
Dying of cancer.

At eighty-six he'd
already buried his parents,
his sister, his wife
of more than fifty years,
all the unborn children
she could never carry to term.
At eighty-six
he was old, tired, ready.
Old, tired, ready.

George Floyd was
forty-six, young, full of youth,
full of life, with a six-year-old
daughter. His family still lives,
his friends still live.
His primary crime?
His skin was black.
Skin was black.

He knew his blue brother—
they worked at the same club—
was personal animosity over some slight,
real or imagined, the reason Derek Chauvin

in his blue-uniformed might
placed his knee on George's neck,
crushed the life out of him?
Why? Why did no one man-up to help?
Why did no one help!

Derek killed his cousin,
for we are all related,
all carry African blood
in our veins, including
the white supremacists.
All of us are colored.
All of us are colored.

Derek placed a knee
on his cousin's neck
gave no mercy
when George begged,
I can't breathe.
Gave no mercy.
No mercy.

And now I cry because
I can't breathe for all my tears.
And now my country cries because
it can't breathe for all its pain
under the knees of the Derek Chauvins.
Knees of the Derek Chauvins.

Is this how the Lokota feel?
Is this how the Navajo feel?
Is this how all Natives feel
as their lands, their lives,

their cultures, die to the knee?
Die to the knee.

Age means little to Death but
must we die with such violence?
Die with such violence?

We. Can't. Breathe.
All my relations.

His Hands: An Ekphrastic Poem Based on A Photograph Not Yet Taken

His walk, slow, deliberate,
each foot placed just so.
Still tall, handsome in a
wild warrior way, faded copper skin,
hair cropped short, uncontrolled. He ignores
the pain as he sits, places the
bag next to him.

He smiles and nods, acknowledges me.
I smile and nod back. We meet like this
most days, never speak, never touch.
He on his bench, me on mine.

His movements determined, labored,
he opens the bag, inserts a hand,
carefully extracts some crackers. He calls—
his voice gravelly, deep—
Henry! Matilda!—Two crows drop
to his bench. He offers
each a cracker.

Absorbed in his world
he does not notice my camera
as it moves to capture
him. And his hands. Rough,
gnarled, the hands of a man
who once worked at hard labor
to provide for himself,

his family. To get through life,
through college, through old age.

The hands of a man
who once could wield a hammer,
build a home, who once could work the machines, the
hellishly hot machines, that turned molten
glass into canning jars. The hands
of a man tender with his woman,
loving with their children, the
hands of a man who
once carried steel in his boot—and knew
how to protect himself,
his family, his people.

The hands of a man,
now crippled by age,
that once held a pen,
wrote essays and poems
for a better life, a better time,
of our people and their tribulations.
Hey Columbus! Are you listening?

One day, he'll come, sit
and I'll have to open the bag
place the crackers in his hand.
But not today. Not today.

        after Thomas Hubbard and his poems

Crow Carries

Crow carries Spirit blankets
woven energy too strong
for the weaver to touch.
She guides the energies
freely given by Spirit animals
for the blanket worn
by the one who needs
using her eyes to move
the energy, weave the energy
untouched until the recipient
wraps it about him.

Crow carries Spirit blankets
each night they are woven
by the woman who sheds tears of love
as she weaves.

Crow carries Spirit blankets
through the heavens
between the stars and moons
delivers blankets
as they are wanted
as they are needed.

Crow carries Spirit blankets
not of his weaving
adds his own stories
adds his own jokes

then laughs
when humans do not understand.

Crow carries Spirit blankets
to those in need
to those in want
does so in joy
does so in love
does so
does so.

Divergence

Does the snowflake remember
skipping on the wind, barely
weighing more than the air
through which it fell
until landing, joining
its siblings, and resting?

Does it remember the cold,
the death-bringing cold
as it became hard, bonded
to its sibs, its lover? Does
it remember the softness of once?

Does the ice remember
the brittleness, the burning cold, the
dark embrace as summer sun
warms it and sends it
down, inexorably down
rushing, gushing meltwater
until it reaches ocean?

Does that water drop, remember
being fresh, pure before mingling
with salt? As it evaporates, rises
to the heavens, does it look
down upon the sea
and long to return?

Does it rejoice as
once again it rides the winds
gathers a particle of dust,
a bit of cold and again
changes shape, again becomes
hexagonal, again rides
the winds, the howling
winds, to the ground
one small snowflake
among billions, having
returned, at last
to the icy welcome of its
one-time lover?

His Bench: An Ekphrastic Poem Based on a Photograph Not Yet Taken

His bench remains empty
these many days.
The sun shines, the rain drizzles
he is not here to call—or feed—
Henry and Matilda.

I sit on his bench
with a bag of crackers
and homemade cookies.
I rattle the bag, call their names—
only stillness.

The view is different
from his bench,
he saw the Salish Sea,
wild waves, dugouts,
young men providing.

I feel his presence,
especially as I look toward
my bench, from where
I looked upon the high desert,
the sage-covered steppes.

I lean against his tree
hold two crackers, close my eyes—
a quiet flutter of wings

a subtle clack of beaks—
the crackers are taken.

He is so close, I can almost
smell him, almost feel him.
My tears fall
in the soft Seattle rain.
I am accepted.

My Death

in response to Erica Jong's poem of the same title

Like Carlos Castaneda,
Erica Jong sees her death
on her left.

It looks like her:
white-skinned, sad-
eyed, thin and pale,
rapidly aging.

But my death is
different. Perhaps
that difference keeps me.

He walks on my
right, pointing out
reasons to laugh,
to live,

teaches me tango,
sings me lullabies,
keeps me warm at night.

My right hand wields
a pen, my left stirs
the pot. Death, my lover,

will carry me in his arms
through the door of
our new home.

Riding with the Assiniboine

Whenever Daddy's body needed a respite,
whenever his mind needed space,
a band of Assiniboine braves only he could see,
who never spoke, brought his horse,
took him riding, then brought him home.

Months passed and the Assiniboine
came less and less often. No longer
did Daddy speak of quiet rides
on the prairie to watch buffalo.
No longer did I hear stories of silent rides
into the hills to hunt antelope or deer.

I still wonder why the Assiniboine came,
Daddy had no Native blood in his veins;
he had never, to my knowledge,
lived in their territory. But they came,
he rode, and lived longer
because of their ministrations.

"Ya know," he said one day,
"I miss my rides with the Assiniboine."
Then came the night all who are born of woman must face,
when he summoned the aides
who took his vitals and called an ambulance,
the night he looked up from his bed, chuckled,
and asked, "Isn't this a hell of a way to go?"

Only Daddy saw the walls dissolve,
the stars burn through winter clouds,
smelled the prairie, heard the horses.
Only the quiet band of braves saw Daddy
rise from his death, mount his horse
and thunder through the heavens as
he rode with the Assiniboine.

Anasazi Blizzard

Highway 550 runs through Cuba, New Mexico.
Best fry bread outside Canyon de Chelly.
Drive north toward Bloomfield, turn left before Nageezi,
go to Chaco—stone pueblos built by Anasazi
without insulation, wallboard or forced air heat.
Abandoned for reasons we can only guess...
a dry creek? Too many rats in the granary?
Clay pots empty of stew? Climate change?

Late spring blizzard robs me of comfort,
steals my warmth. I long for the welcoming
heat of fires that once burned in the now empty
stone rooms. I long for surcease from the pain
of wind-whipped snow. I yearn for the perfume
of stews that haven't been cooked here in generations.
I listen to the wind and hear happy shrieks
of children who played in these homes centuries ago;
I listen to the wind and hear raucous calls of
bright-plumed birds—ghosts on their cold, empty perches.

Sunlight does not exist, only biting,
stinging snow that slams into silent
kivas waiting to hear ancient prayers
in an ancient language
no one speaks, no one remembers.
Highway 550 still runs through Cuba.

Once Upon A Time...

For Tony Hillerman

> *I had a little boy*
> *a long time ago*
> *.Johnny was his*
> *name*

I had a Ma
till I was 'most eleven.
Then Frank moved in.
He drank.
He beat Ma and me.

> *Johnny was a good boy*
> *but Frank didn't like him.*
> *Frank was bone-deep mean*
> *used to beat Johnny*
> *run him off.*

A
JURY
OF
YOUR
PEERS

I'd hide in the neighbor's
garage
till they sent me
back.

                              HAS

                           FOUND

                             YOU

                          GUILTY

                                        Once, Johnny ran away
                                          from Frank's fists
                                             and belt,

State didn't care.

                              OF

                          MURDER

                                        and Frank, he upped
                                       and moved us away

Ma asked Frank
for some of her
welfare money
to buy me a present
I was gonna be eleven.

                              IN

                             THE

                           FIRST

                          DEGREE.

                                         He wouldn't let
                                          me go back
                                          or nuthin'

Frank hit her.
Took his belt off
and come for me.
I ran.
Ma screamedand

Frank whipped her.
Ma cried.

YOU

SHALL

BE

HANGED

When I cried for my boy
Frank beat me.
Put me in the
hospital more'n' once.

State didn't care.

BY

THE

NECK

Last time I saw Johnny
was just before he
turned eleven.

I went home
on my birthday.
Thought maybe Ma
would let me in,
give me sumthin'
to eat.
I was hungry
And scared.

He was runnin' from Frank.
Made Frank mad,
so he beat on me.
I never saw Johnny again.
Never got to say I was sorry.
Never got to tell him good-bye.

Home was gone.
Frank done hitched
the trailer to his
truck and drove away.

UNTIL

DEAD.

If you find my Ma
tell her I still love her.
I been lookin' for her
all these years.

*I had a little boy
once,
a long time ago.*

But, now,
the state cares.

Othello the African

From a photo of a tombstone in a pre-Revolutionary War cemetery

The churchyard holds tombstones, many
dated before the Revolutionary War.

Crowded, they slump at various
angles, shade each other, protect

each other from feuds
long forgotten. A congenial glut of

love and laughter, now heard only
by the dead as they tumble

together. All but one, ostracized and
alone. Othello the African,

had a family, then another
and another — who knew how

many? Loved by all he is also
here, with his own engraved stone.

Just not too near, for he
was loved, just not enough.

David Malin Cortez

David Malin Cortez, child of a Spanish fur trapper
and a Native mother, not wanted by either, or grandmother.
Three, maybe four years old, neglected, burned, cut, tortured

when given to and adopted by Narcissa and Marcus Whitman.
At Waiilatpu, he learned not just acceptance but love, play
not torture. It was short-lived happiness. He was kidnapped with

the other metis children by Joe Finley so they wouldn't die
with the whites, the family David loved, who loved him.
Come back. Come back.

Taken to the Jesuits at old Fort Walla Walla
where the Walla Walla and Columbia rivers meet,
the priests kept him, threatened him

with sale to the Cayuse as a slave, or return
to his birth mother—either choice a death sentence.
Peter Skene Ogden ransomed the white captives

still at Waiilatpu, brought them to the fort—Davey again
knew love and family for his sisters, Mary Ann Bridger
and the Sager girls—now free and alive came to take him with

them to Oregon City. They brought his bible, a gift from
Mother Narcissa when adopted, when baptized. They held
him in their arms. Told him of their love.

He reveled in their love. Cried when told
who died, especially his sister, Helen Mar Meek.
Come back. Come back.

He wept at his loss but had family. Again.
Until the boats loaded. The men shoved him off
kept him from his sisters, would not let him journey

with his family to Portland, to Oregon City.
No adult wanted him. His skin was too dark.
His color matched the mud flat on which he stood.

Though heavy with pain, his heart filled with light, he called
Come back. Come back. Take me with you.
His beloved sisters tried to get the boats turned around.

They begged, they pleaded. *Go back. Go back. Please, go
back.*
How do you tell an eight-year-old sobbing, heartbroken child
no one wants him because of his **color**? His only family

of love, dead, buried, or disappeared forever down river.
His little heart, filled with love for his family, became so bright
he glowed. The priests feared this love, his literacy,

stole the bible given him by Mother Narcissa
brought by his sisters to read, to have. Alone, unloved,
unwanted by all around him, his heart-light dimmed, went out.

His sister, Helen Mar Meek, dead from lack of succor as she lay
dying of measles, found him, took his hand. They walked
away from the darkness, were welcomed by the light.

Come back. Come back.

Solitude in Spring Rain

The house is quiet.
Through the glass I watch birds
feed as if they hadn't eaten since
forever. They call their
flock-mates to join them
bobbing their heads to the
syncopated rhythm
of my mind song.

A day of promise, filled with steady
gray Seattle rain interrupted
by bright flashes of color –
red-winged blackbirds, finches
in shiny purple and bold yellow.

I watch the rain, a shimmer
of silver threads, undulate
across the emerald grass.

Used to the rain, the birds dive in
a blur of feathers to the feeders, scarcely
acknowledge their mates while
they eat and keep watchful eyes out
for the neighbor's ubiquitous gray cat.

By tomorrow, my upturned
lawn chairs will be impromptu birdbaths.
Today, raindrops turn them into
a thousand mini-fountains.

Like solitude, silence is
an illusion. The winds shift;
rain beats a soft tattoo against the glass.

Soon, a warrior, plumed in gaudiness
he hopes will attract a mate,
bursts through my door.

This While

I lie next to you this night
listen to your soft snores
feel your chest move up
move down, enjoy your
body so close to mine

and fear this is
our last time together.

A thousand miles and more
separate our homes; I fear
you won't return,
and I cannot come to you.

Age holds us both
in an iron grip; only one way
for us to break free.

I so want to share
with you the years we have left
to treasure you,
to hold you close and tell you
I love you—
but your heart belongs
to the Sea.

If you ask, will the Sea call me,
allow me to be with you?
You and she have years

together; a history you and I
can never share.

I swing between happiness
you have her to love
and tears it is not me.

I do not sleep while we are
together; I lie awake
listen to your soft breaths
feel your chest move up,
move down
          keep you
covered so you don't chill
as you dream of that distant sea
and marvel
you chose me

for at least this while.

Grandpa's Walnut Trees

Voracious flames leap
from torch to faery-built cocoon
suspended from Grandpa's walnut trees.

Fuzzy caterpillars
roasted alive, their death shrieks
heard as spluttering hisses.

Faery ash whirls on the wind
a little girls' tears puddle the sidewalk.
She grieves a loss she'll never understand.

What Good is Your Love?

Place your son's name here.
Place your daughter's name here.

Write your mother's name in this space.
Write your father's name here.

Do you have nieces? Nephew's?
Write their names here.

And here   and here.
Aunts? Uncles? Add their names.

Grandparents? Friends? More kith
or kin? Make a list of all their names

Make it long. Make it with love. Make it
legible. Take your time. Fill a page with names.

Fill two pages. Three if need be. All the people
you know and love. Tack the pages

to a wall. Look at them. Study them.
Have you recently told them of your

love? Why not? They all may die
tomorrow. Shot at work. At school.

In the mall. On the street. In their bed.
Wherever. What good is your love

without action? How many of *your* family,
your friends, *your* relations must die

too soon before *you* act?

Little Boys and War

I was six; brother was five.
Papa was gone to war.
Planes roared overhead
racing for the city,
Our farmhouse shook;
dishes crashed to the floor.

Mama screamed and
called us to her.
In the roar, we refused to hear,
and rushed outside
to watch the show.

Did we really see the bombs
fly toward the city?
"There! There!" we'd yell in delight
planes swooshed low,
dirt blossomed upward,
lives destroyed,
for our enjoyment.

And mama screamed
and called us to her bosom.
This time, we answered to her tears.
"But, Mama," we'd explain,
"It's so exciting!"

Mama Said

He zooms up on his
motorcycle, offers us
candy and a ride—
if we come *right now.*

"Your Mama said
it's okay."

Brother sits in front
of the sidecar
and I sit in back.
Over my shoulder

I see Mama running
fast, her mouth open
wide, her arms
stretched out to us.

*From a photo of two young boys looking back out of a
motorcycle car*

Escape impossible in sunlight

the wall above me,
pocked by random bullets, says
"Welcome to Sarajevo."

On the tarmac
wounded by ricocheted
fragments of "Welcome,"

I pray.

The Bride's Gate

Loops, finely wrought of iron,
interlocked one upon the other,
painted a soft, warm green
beckons, "Welcome."
The gate allows
errant breezes to pass
through the thick stone wall.
Hinges, rusted, are swung
only for entrance
of a new bride.

Frightened, alone,
she meets her husband
for the first time
within the garden,
through the second,
and inner gate;
the bride's gate,
closely wrought in
opposing patterns,
flat bars of prison
deep, earth brown.

No light or laughter
escapes the gates.
Only the errant breeze,
her prayers, and
eventually, her ashes.

From **The Unfound Doo**r, at the Community Bridge in Frederick, Maryland

Dachau, KZ Gedankstädte*

Well-tailored paths
laid with German precision
intersect villages
where millions lived
and died.

Perfect right angles,
paths divide
at front and back doors
parallel walled boundaries.
Trod once, path gravel

remains forever
in my craw
to help digest history
into a non-repeatable meal.

I walked those paths
one warm, breezeless day
the laughter of children
tumbled through the walls,
I heard mournful agonies of

Gypsies and Jews and
Christians and Other Undesirables.
My knees jellied
as I toured the museum,
wept at photos and letters and
shoes of my

never-to-be known family.
I prayed to their same
deaf god, begged the same
burning questions, received the same
mute response.

The Exit
is still through the crematorium.

*a place you will never forget
literal translation: Concentration camp memorial

Waiting Outside a Village in Viet Nam

from White Badge: A Novel of Korea, by Ahn Junghyo

In the tent, smoking an
American cigarette
the old man sat on his heels
studied the GIs with

a steady gaze.
When he finally asked
in perfect French
only one GI could
understand his quiet words.

"When," he barely whispered,
"will you go home
so we can plant and
harvest and
live in peace, again?"

Surprised, the Liberator asked
"Don't you want us to
defeat the enemy, first?"
"No," he wheezed, "It
doesn't matter who wins.

They still have to eat
and we, my village,
are very tired of all this war.

We just want to
plant and harvest

what is ours.
The Cong steals.
The ARVN steals.
You Amis steal.
We have nothing left."

Quiet in the tent, his sad
dark eyes focused on a happier past.
He smoked to the filter,
stood to leave,
and asked for one more cigarette.

The Tranquil Sound

The basin lay
as though carelessly tossed
catching sun light
in its glass interior,
light dancing from
blister-bumps
to age-vein cracks;
filled with waters that sough
with the tides
and serenade the moon.

Breezes dance
tiny paths in the dust
seen only by the circling Roc,
who cries to the emptiness below.

The basin lay
as it had for years
lost to all but the Roc

        and the lonely soldier,
        sentinel on the edge of glass
        whose glowing skeleton
        still clutches rust
        that once was weapon;
        faithfully watching
        with eyeless sockets
        the once tree filled

hunting grounds
of old Chief Sealth.

Foolish lad. Dead.
Defending a people who wanted
no defense.

     Still, the circling Roc cries.

Comanche Butte, Texas

I remember Granbury, Texas as flat
clouds scudding across the pale blue sky.
I remember Comanche Butte as
dark, table-topped, bereft of trees,
a mountain beheaded by a scimitar of the gods
the head thrown far away. I was nine
when I visited, heard the story.

Two families, my ancestors, not knowing or not caring,
made homesteads on holy, sacred Comanche ground.
They farmed—one on top of the butte and one below,
a desecration the Comanche could not ignore.
Angered, they killed the family below,
in full view of the family above who knew
their fortune fled on the backs of circling buzzards.
Without escape they vowed to take
many a Comanche with
them as escort to meet their Maker.

Retired to their cabin, heated by the sun
in summer, by the cook stove in winter,
they loaded their weapons, talked, prayed,
and waited. And waited. And then they
waited some more.

Deep ethereal silence rose up the butte
on wings of doves to announce
the Comanche vanished, the dead,

scattered upon the ground, waited
for eternity, waited for burial.

I still see the killing when I sleep.
I still hear the screams. I still
wave good-bye to my cousin, held by
a Comanche brave, her blonde hair wraps
about him as they ride to an uncertain future, a home
of clouds scudding across the pale blue sky.

Because It Is Waiilatpu,

after Tony Hoagland

the winds come through the valley
carry the death songs of those who lost

their blood upon the ground. You must be still
to hear their songs, and even then the words
are in a language only the dead can understand.

Because it is Waiilatpu, little
Alice Clarissa runs and tumbles, laughs

with the exuberance of a two-year-old toddler,
through the purple rye, to play with the other ghosts

not understanding their weeping, not understanding their death.

Because It is Waiilatpu,
covered in emerald grass, turtles nest by the mill pond
deer wander through the replaced orchard

winds carry the dust and grit of plowed fields
the perfumes of sage and wheat, grape and rye.

The ghosts use the winds and the grit to polish the marble slab
to high sheen, knowing when their names are obliterated
they will at last be free.

Because *this* is Waiilatpu.

I, Empath

 receive your pains
your hurts, your agonies
onto my plate; eat them—
accept them, digest them
allow them into
my body, my psyche.

The agony of a dying child,
the pain of impending bankruptcy,
the ache of a disabled spouse,
the anger of loss as you die
millimeter by millimeter,
the constant rat-teeth nausea of fear
loss of hope, loss of love,
as we await that inevitability.

You do not ask
if I am hungry,
if I would like a plate
of your pains, your agonies,
you assume—
and stuff me full of your empty calories
before you hang up, sign off, drive away.

How do I diet these unsightly pounds
I am forced by friendship, by love
to carry wherever I go?
Who do *I* talk to? On whose shoulder
do *I* cry? Who is *my* Empath?

Life in Slow Motion

He gets out of bed, shuffles to the kitchen,
pours his coffee, his milk, stands in the door
deciding whether to sit at the table or
shuffle to the sofa.

Conversations are odd. They begin
mid-sentence, he pauses, his mind
goes over what he was saying, what he might say,
does he really deserve a bowl of ice cream?

Pain does weird things; it pulls us,
bends us, requires us to always acknowledge it,
take meds to placate it,
take meds to dull it, to dull us.

The fractured sternum heals, that pain lessens
as he holds the pillow close to cough.
The arthritis in his neck continues to grow; slow,
deliberate, causes excruciating pain in his back.

More pain—slower movements,
more pills, more patches, more moans. More thoughts
slide in on quiet clouds of Morpheus, perhaps
a life in slow motion isn't a life at all.

Saving Against Alzheimer's

How do you save your nouns and your verbs?
Do you write them in a notebook and keep it with you?
Do you tie them in brightly colored silk scarves?

A blue scarf for water, as it flows upon the rocks,
under the bridge, fills the river, sings of love
and sorrow. Knot it about your neck. Do not forget.

Take your red scarf, the color of blood, the color of life.
Into it put memories of your babies, your husband,
the war he didn't survive. Knot it, twice. Do not lose.

Your white scarf holds your prayers and tears, the
mourning of what might have been but can never be.
Gather your sadness, remember it, respect it. Tie the knot tight.

Fill your yellow scarf with happiness. The bliss
of laughing babies, your first published poem,
happy times with good friends, the joys of discovery.

Knot that scarf over your heart; hold it tight. Keep the good nouns close, the happy verbs a part of your life. Hold onto the scarves, the knots, as you sail off the bridge.

Your nouns and your verbs will survive.

Inspired by the South Korean movie, *Poetry*. For more about the film, please go to:
http://asianmediawiki.com/Poetry_%282010-South_Korean_Movie%29

Awaiting Death

Awaiting death
of friends in days
or weeks, or maybe even months
I find it hard
to care about
squabbles and pains
that one does nothing to alleviate
or the financial problems
they chose, and clutch
to their bosom—
a mother holding her babies
tight to her loving breast—
in fear they might escape.

Awaiting death
in days, or weeks, or maybe even months
if luck prevails and no pain is involved
I find myself re-evaluating friends
who over-use my shoulders
my sympathetic ears
as if owned—
bought and paid for by their
ever growing need—
with no concern as to whether
my bones are strong enough
for the added weight.
Their slave, I must listen.
tut-tut in mindless obedience.

Awaiting death
in days, or weeks, or maybe even months,
I light joss
chant, find what peace
I can in repetition of sound
in breathing in and breathing out
in accepting all is illusion—
that some illusions
are sadder than others—
that death is an
integral part of life.

Awaiting your death
in days, or weeks, or maybe even months
I know I do not want you to leave.
Ever. I am selfish, I
do not want to accept
life's inevitable turn.
I weep and want my tears
now, to count for something;
know more will come
in days, or weeks, or maybe even months
when I must release
a part of my very life
when I must say good-bye
when mourning will overtake
my illusions
when the wheel of life
will begin its new cycle.

No Time for Death

There are cemeteries that are lonely. —Pablo Neruda

Lonely cemeteries
are not filled with men.
Men understand Death. Men have
camaraderie. Men stand for hours
at the bar, raise whiskey to their lips
and drink. Men salute Death.

Only men know Death.
Only men stand at the bar.
Only men die wearing
their boots. Their best boots.
Men die in company with friends.
They do not die alone. They are
not buried in a lonely cemetery.

Women do not stand at the bar.
They do not drink whiskey.
They do not salute Death.
They do not understand Death.

Women understand Life.
They understand birthing and bathing.
They clean. They sow. They reap.
They mend. They cook. They preserve.
Women are too busy for Death.
At rest in lonely cemeteries,
women are grateful.

I Couldn't Find Their Names

"If you can survive Basic Training, you can survive anything..."
—SFC Annie B. Hawkins, USWAC Recruiter
...war, pestilence, childbirth...

On my walk this Memorial Day
I collect memories—as a butterfly bush
collects butterflies—
soft, bright, never still,
never in sharp focus.

I remember WAC Basic Training
I remember Lieutenant Graham
who taught Military Customs and Courtesies.
She, alone, treated us as humans deserving respect.
She shared stories of her affianced—
a Green Beret Captain in Viet Nam—
a Hero. To all others we were,
at best, lowly enlisted swine.

I try to hold
the happier memories—
all female recruits with
bottle blonde hair
were told to wait until after Basic
to touch up their roots.
Really? Have you ever known
a bottle blonde to allow her roots to show?
We knew them the minute they exited

the chlorine gas chamber,
their hair a lovely shade
of Army-issued green.

We stood at attention
for the Star Spangled Banner
while attending the 14th Army Band (WAC)
Christmas concert 16 December '65.
The rocket's red glare
met Lieutenant Graham and me in 'Nam
where we saw the death
heard the death
smelled the death
of her hero—a Captain in the Green Berets.
She, too, died in-country that night
when, behind her quarters
on Fort McClellan, Alabama,
she chose her 'cide
with her Army–issued .45.

Some nightmares
refuse to fade with daylight.
Some hells refuse to dissipate
no matter what god is followed,
no matter what god is beseeched.

It still hurts to hear our
National Anthem.

I visited The Wall.
Searched the listing for
Green Beret, Captain, Hero.
Couldn't find a listing for

WAC, Lieutenant Graham, Hero, either.
I looked for both. They were not there.

I remember Bugs as small, wiry
wearing coke-bottle glasses.
Possibly nineteen
probably eighteen
a natural comedian
he was fun and laughter
until snuggly wrapped
in the tight VC tunnel he, too,
met the rocket's red glare.

I never found him
on The Wall, either. No one there
named Bugs.

I married, went to Germany.
Two years later, pregnant,
I accepted my discharge,
worried about my husband
in the 101st Air Borne Division
Cam Ranh Bay, Viet Nam.

We later divorced, married others, he retired
from the Army, died of too many coffin nails.
'Nam killed him, too, years before he died.
His name isn't on Our Wall, either.

It still hurts to hear our
National Anthem.

Young Lions of an Indifferent Pride

On the bottom shelf—four high school
yearbooks, fifty years unopened. Pages
of smiling faces, innocent, expectant,

boys I once knew. Bottom shelf boys,
college not an option. Raised to work, to
respect their elders, raised on a goodly dose

of John Wayne movies. Young lions of an
indifferent pride, they laughed their way
through Basic Training. They learned to shoot,

they learned to kill, they learned to play
the game, to win the war, to get the babes.
Still filled with bravado and laughter

they shipped out to 'Nam and learned
to fear, learned to die. Bottom shelf men
who now exist in a granite wall.

A Marvelous Age

I am seventy-seven and a half years old.
That half, at my age, is important.
Like the small child who raises fingers
and proudly proclaims to one and all,
I am this many years and two *days.*
I gather all the days
the weeks, the months I can
to make another year.

Actuaries tell me
I'll live to be eighty-six—
ten years older than my closest relative
at the time of his death—
but that was before
the Novel Coronavirus moved
next door. Now we all count
disease-free days right
along with body counts—
both numbers go inexorably higher.
One much faster than the other.

My children are healthy—
I don't see them—
we talk on the phone, text.
My friends are healthy—
I don't see them, either—
we video conference
acknowledge proper social distancing
as we share happy hour

separated by screens, by walls,
by states, by miles.

I am seventy-seven years
six months, one week, two days old,
strive for one more day
one more month
one more year.

Holy Lands

What makes land holy?
Is it the people who lived on it
who loved it, who died
protecting it, their families,
their loved ones buried there?

All land is holy land. All land contains
the dead, the memories, the salt of tears.

Is it the people who still live there,
who care for the land, who respect
the land of their birth,
the land of their mothers,
the land of their elders?

The people who work the land, who respect it,
who feed it their blood and sweat make it holy.

Perhaps it is the mythology
that one or more of their gods
was born there, died there,
resurrected there,
and never saw a reason to leave?

We invent gods from our longings;
beg for their blessings.

Maybe that the Grandfathers and Grandmothers
carved it, stacked it, furrowed it,

colored it with white and brown, purple and green,
red and yellow—painted the lands
their favorite colors?

All land provides for those who live on it,
respect what it offers.

What makes a land holy?
I don't know—but I know
when I stand on it and the world goes hush
and I hear the holy song, think the holy thoughts,
and know the love of all my relations.

When we die, we give back to the land what we've taken—
blood, bone, ash. The circle continues, unbroken.

Marking the Hours

A Personal Essay in Poetic Form

...and I look upon time as no more than an idea,
and I consider eternity as another possibility,
—Mary Oliver, "When Death Comes"

11:30 p.m.

> *All a sane man can care about*
> *is giving love.*
>
> —Hafiz

I tuck the blanket under Uncle's chin,
lean over to kiss him good night.
Don't go, he says, *I don't have*
much longer, his voice barely a whisper.
I pull the chair close,
hold his hand, and watch Death's
tentative approach, wary of his welcome,
see him with great respect
slide into Uncle's body, a little here,
a little there, until, until …

Deliberately, Uncle picks objects
from the air, moves them
from one side of the bed
to the other, sets them down gently
on tables only he can see.

I see those large, strong hands
bait a hook, help his young
niece toss the line into the water. I
feel those same hands
wipe tears from my face
when I caught nothing.

4:00 a.m.

> *maybe death*
> *isn't darkness, after all,*
> *but so much light*
> *wrapping itself around us—*
> *as soft as feathers—*

—Mary Oliver, "White Owl
Flies Into and Out of the Field"

He asks for cereal. I make his favorite,
Maypo. He eats two bites, that's all.
Now he eats dreams instead of cookies,
drinks memories instead of juice.
He converses with unseen beings
in an unintelligible language
about unknown issues.

It's foggy, he declares. How can he
tell? I look through the window; it's
black as tar outside.

Why, here comes the Skipper!
Happy excitement in his voice.
His father, my grandpa, has been dead
for years. He carries on a lengthy
conversation, with pauses while Grandpa
speaks. Maybe I can learn from these talks,
get an insider's view from the other side?
When the conversation ceases,
I ask what Grandpa said, and Uncle replies,
Oh, he said, 'bfllgmffg'. So much for
hearing from the dead.

10:30 a.m.

> "...what happens at the point of death?"
> Raven sat silently for a while, then said,
> "I give away my belongings."
>
> —Robert Aitken, *Zen Master Raven*

The Hospice nurse arrives,
tells me he is *actively dying*,
whatever the hell that means.

I put a CD in the player, soft
flute music for meditation fills my corner
of the room. I tell myself this will ease him
on his journey. I lie. I play it for me. I need
the comfort, the strength.

His old cat, Scrub, the Empress
Dowager (Bitch!) Cat of the Universe
died in his arms yesterday.
Brave little thing.
She gave him necessary permission,
then showed him *how.*
If he just *would.*

His breaths sound
like soft open-mouth snores
more noted by their absence.
I want to burn a candle
help him walk in light,
I want to burn incense
so he can breathe perfumed air

but fear to aggravate
his emphysema

Scrub will be cremated.
He will be cremated.
Their ashes, mixed,
then scattered upon the
waters with those of his wife
of 50 plus years.

Critters die much easier
than people. Why are we
so sure we're the

higher life form?

And time continues along the Möbius loop.
Only my perceptions of death, of life, change.

1:13 p.m.

> *Here is*
> *a test to find*
> *whether your mission on earth*
> *is finished:*
> > *If you're alive,*
> > *it isn't.*
>
> —Richard Bach, *Illusions*

He fights, *Can't breathe*.
I raise his head two, maybe three inches.
He sighs with contentment,
slips back into shallow, fitful sleep.
He breathes again.

1:36 p.m.

> *Goodbyes are only for those who love with*
> *their eyes. Because for those who love with*
> *their heart and soul there is no such thing*
> *as separation.*
>
> —Rumi

Watching him,
I feel so helpless.
I can neither hold him back,
nor speed him on.
I grump at Grandpa
for being so damnably slow
in taking him on this final journey.

But then, I yelled at god
for the same thing when he
took his sweet, slow, and tardy time
in taking my Auntie Marie.

I hope when my turn arrives
I will grasp it with more eagerness
and less fear.

I burned cedar and sweet grass
for Scrub. Said prayers.
Thanked her for being—
and cried like she was my
best friend. Maybe she was.

Suki, the Puppy Princess of the Universe
plays with a ball in his room

as he struggles to let go.
Strong affirmation that Life
is part of the continuing Cycle
of the Cauldron.

I tell Uncle to find Grandpa,
take his hand,
go with him.

I've known this man, my mother's brother,
my only uncle, all my life. We laughed together
over shaggy dog stories, we held each other

as we cried when family and friends died.
Never again
will his arms comfort me.

He taught me to fish, to laugh at myself.
Now, I must teach him—to die.
I don't know how.

4:00 p.m.

Fire cools.
Water seeks its own level
> —Deng Ming-Dao,
> *365 Tao Daily Meditations*

He still gets his meds for pain.
Better dying through chemistry.
He quiets, I doze. Need sleep.
Can't sleep. Too tired.
Will sleep soon—too soon.

He skips more breaths.
His skin heats as his internal
thermostat breaks down and dies.

I find myself holding
my breath as he forgets to breathe.
Is death a reversal
of the birthing process—I wonder
does long labor correlate
to long dying?

Page after page
of random thoughts
relating to mortality—
is there hidden herein
a poem?

And time continues along the Möbius loop.
Only my perceptions of death, of life, change.

6:45 p.m.

> *I have one more task to do—*
> —Maxine Hong Kingston,
> *I Love A Broad Margin to My Life*

I eat dinner in his room,
raise a glass of single malt scotch—
his favorite—and offer a toast:
L'Chaim! To Life!

I urge him to turn loose of this life,
to leave his body, his pain,
to go with Grandpa.
I urge him to find his new life, *L'Chaim*!

Memories of family dinners
flood in with that toast. Holidays,
and the true meaning of a "groaning
board"—but mostly, I remember
the hot pastrami sandwiches
I brought from his favorite deli
and the good conversations we had
on topics ranging from the stock market
to how to paint landscapes to dying and death.

7:43 p.m.

...ask yourself the crucial question, "What
would I have done?"

—Simon Wiesenthal, *The Sunflower*

I leave the room for a few minutes.
My son and fiancé are with him.
He is not alone; he is not without love.
Yet, he waits for just this time.

The Hospice nurse had told me he
probably would wait until I
left the room. Her words were wise.

8:06 p.m.

Our death is our wedding with eternity.
—Rumi

I return.
His breathing stopped.
His heart stopped.
No pulse.
No life.

And time continues along the Möbius loop.
Only my perceptions of death, of life, change.

8:10 p.m.

What the caterpillar
calls the end of the world
the master calls a
butterfly

—Richard Bach, *Illusions*

I call Hospice.
The duty nurse is an old and dear friend.
She comes, holds me while I cry.
My home, now empty of Uncle,
is but a hollow shell.

My childhood officially
ended I am now Family Matriarch.
The responsibility for family
has shifted from his large shoulders
to my small ones. It is now up
to me to give comfort, not take it.
I cry for my loss.
Alone, I try to say "Good-bye."
Do tears speak loud enough
to be heard by the dead?

11:30 p.m.

You only lose what you cling to.
           —Buddha

Alone, even though
my son and fiancé are here,
I sleep in the strange quiet,
knowing I no longer
must listen for him
to ring the bell, call me to his side.
My presence
no longer required.

One more night and he could have
welcomed in the new year,
the new century. He looked forward
to the extravagant celebrations.
It is hard to join the celebrations
without him.

The Next Day.

I clean, go through his things,
I organize. I cry.
The tears cleanse my heart
as I empty his closet.

I pull his flannel shirts from the
hangers, wrap myself
in their comfort, cherish
the last scent of him. Smile at the paint
stains—the blues, the greens, the reds—
of the landscapes he loved to paint:
Mount Shuksan,* his favorite model,
from the front, the back, either side.
I hope others will find these shirts,
these stains, and be inspired
as they wear them.
Trousers, socks—all go into
the wash. All are cleaned,
folded, donated.

The handkerchiefs, I keep.
I photograph Uncle's paintings—they
will be given to family
and friends. His paints and
brushes I keep. Memories of him
pulled close, wrapped around me,
a blanket of love that smells faintly
of linseed oil and turpentine.

Choked with tears,
I can't breathe.
Can't breathe, I now remember,
    were his last words.

And time continues along the Möbius loop.
Only my perceptions of death, of life, change.
    All our perceptions of death, of life, change.

To live in this world
you must be able
    to do three things:
    to love what is mortal;
    to hold it

    against your bones knowing
    your own life depends on it;
    and, when the time comes to let it go,
    to let it go.

                —Mary Oliver,
                "In Blackwater Woods"

---

*Mount Baker, North Cascades, Washington State

At The Beach

(After Uncle Carl's Death)

i.

Black sky.
Black water.
Only horizontal lines
Of phosphorescent horses
Charging the shore
Keep them
From becoming
One.

ii.

A glow in the clouds
The moon beckons

iii.

Little lights on the dark beach glow –
Garbage reflecting unseen light?
Or sea creatures phosphorescing
As they decay?

iv.

White line at the
Water's edge -

Luminescent rope of pearls
Keep the horses at bay.
They dive under the sand,
Swim back to sea
To try another landing.

v.

Glenfiddich from a
Ceramic coffee mug
Better that
Than a plastic cup!

vi.

A drop of Glenfiddich remains
To be poured into the ocean
On the morrow.
Tonight I drink
All but the drop
And hopefully sleep
Until the morrow.

vii.

A hundred
Headless seagulls
Parade on the
Snow covered beach.

viii.

Do I see birds
Bobbing in the breakers?
Or seals playing
In the gray green sea?
Or souls of drowned sailors
Trying to escape
their watery grave?

Acknowledgements

A most heartfelt *Thank You* to Sharmagne Leland-St John for editing this collection. She was gentle in her edits—but firm. It is because of her this book exists.

2,075 Possible Tickets to Eternity first appeared in Arnazella Literary Magazine 1995, and later in a collection by the author, Confessions of a Peace Monger, 1998

Mary Oliver Wants to Die When it's Raining and *His Hands* have both been accepted for publication by Quill and Parchment Online Literary Journal.

Little Boys and War first published in *Cradle Songs: An Anthology of Poetry on Motherhood* 2012, Winner of the 2013 International Book award 2013 (Quill and Parchment Press), in the blog Oddsnbods.com, April 2017

Mama Said, First Prize winner, Issue #22, Tattoo Highway Magazine, Fall 2011 http://www.tattoohighway.org/22/lgcontest.html

Life in Slow Motion, first appeared in Whispers… an international online journal, February 27, 2016

Saving Against Alzheimer's, forthcoming in The Chrysalis Project anthology, 2022; first published by Whispers… an international online journal, May 23, 2014

Othello the African first published by Bulletpen, an African online literary magazine, March 2013

Waiting Outside a Village in Viet Nam appeared in a collection by the author, Confessions of a Peace Monger, 1998

This While first published by Five Willows Literary Review, May 2020

Grandpa's Walnut Trees first published by Heliocentric Net, 1993

The Tranquil Sound first published in There Will Be War VIII: Armageddon!, 1989, later in WestWind the magazine of Norwescon, and in a collection by the author, Confessions of a Peace Monger, 1998

Because It Is Waiilatpu, first published in WA129, Poems Selected by Tod Marshall Washington State Poet Laureate, 2016-2018

Marking the Hours. An earlier version of this poem was used as part of a sermon on death and dying at Evergreen Unitarian Universalist Church in 2000.

About Marking the Hours

This is really a personal essay in poetic form. My uncle lived his final months with me, and because I was tired when he asked me to sit with him that night (the only time he did so), I grabbed my notebook, and kept track of the hours, through which he slept most of the time. It was done more to keep me awake and for the hospice nurse when she would come in a few more hours. I truly didn't know it was the end of his life.